THE
EMOTIONAL
CODE

Mastering Communication in the Digital Age of AI

DR. ETEL LEIT

Published by SignShine™
Text and illustrations Copyright ©2024 by Dr. Etel Leit

UnAddicted to You
ISBN: 978-0-9885952-8-6

For more information regarding permission contact www.DrEtelLeit.com

Printed in the United States of America

To my siblings
Liat Sharon, Libby,
Shmulik & Sasi -
you're each my special shining star.

Table of Contents

Part A:
The Digital Era: The Role of Technology in Our Lives

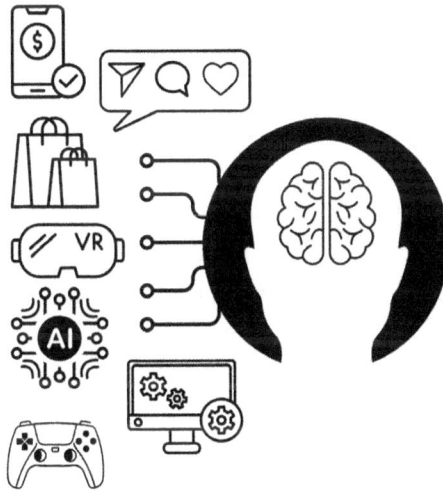

IS THIS WHAT YOUR MIND
LOOKS LIKE?

livia is a 24-year-old college student attending university. She lives in the dorms with her best friend. Some of her classes are online, so she has taken some time to adjust to her new daily schedule. As soon as she wakes up, she checks social media and scrolls through her feed liking posts. The star from her favorite TV show announces a new film they're in, and a new dance trend video are her first likes of the morning. Her friend's party last night, a flier for her upcoming fundraising event, and a new selfie of her ex-boyfriend all pop up on her screen and flood her mind before she gets ready to start her day. Her eyes still feel heavy, so she orders coffee through an app on her phone before she begins school. Olivia parks herself at her desk for the day once she has her coffee because her class assignments, grades, and discussions can all be done online.

She looks at her online calendar, and remembers her graduation is coming up fast! Olivia heads to her favorite job search website to update her professional resume and profile. Her mom texts her to check up on her and ask how she's doing, but Olivia already feels stressed by the day, so she rushes to respond with an emotionless text back "Kk." To take a break from working all morning and afternoon, she swipes through her dating app hoping someone will catch her eye. Her break quickly turns to anxiety when she finally finds a match and begins to worry if this could be her next love or her next heartbreak.

Olivia notices another reminder, which she usually ignores. This time it is for her meditation app which she pays monthly for, but never uses. Something about having a membership removes her guilt. She starts to meditate, but then she hears a ping, she peeps to see what the ping is and realizes she needs to submit homework in two hours. Meditation is canceled for now.

Olivia has two hours to write a 10-page paper. She opens ChatGTP hoping to finalize her masterpiece. She is already overwhelmed. *BING!* Her phone lights up with a coupon for pizza delivery! She promised she will start eating healthy today, but the price is too good to pass up. Olivia orders pizza for dinner to be sent to her dorm, she adds cheese sticks and soda because they have an extra special. Eating healthy is postponed till tomorrow.

Olivia's brain is flooded. She checks her dating app one more time, and contemplated taking new pictures tomorrow to show her better figure. She can always edit the curves. Overwhelmed and feeling not so good about the pizza she ate, Olivia needs a little distraction, something to make her feel good, so she indulges in retail therapy, scrolling though shopping apps and filling up her carts before she closes her eyes and falls asleep.

This is the reality of our current generation, where every aspect of life is involved in technology. We are given technology so early without being taught how to properly use it, it's like being given a car without learning how to drive it. How are we expected to succeed without proper guidance? In this book we delve into how technology impacts us every day and how to use emotional digital literacy to equip us with success in this new life in a digital era.

Chapter 1:

Reshaping Realities: Digital Metamorphosis

From Stone Age to Silicon Age: The Evolution of Technology

From the stone age to our silicone age, we have witnessed exponential advancements in technology that has led us to seamlessly integrate it in our everyday lives. The evolution has been nothing but remarkable as it introduced lightning-fast computers, compact smartphones, and the ever-evolving internet. Can you imagine a world without these creations? Responsibilities, activities, interactions and much more we engage in daily would be impossible without the technology we are familiar with today.

While we have a general understanding of technology, many of us are unable to form an exact definition or describe where it came from. The concept of "digital" is information that is represented in a discrete form. This form is often binary, meaning it uses digits as representation. Technologies have evolved over time, and it's important to recognize these evolutions have a starting point and how they were key steps that led us to the modern digital age. While the first type of technology were tools and weapons in the stone age, technology took a new meaning in the start of a digital age, where computing systems and computers took the spotlight.

As more discoveries are made, more people are drawn to the technological marvels that aid us so well in what we need and want to achieve. An astonishing 4.95 billion people worldwide are a part of the technological era we are in, with an average 600,000 new users joining every day. But, it seems we, and the millions of people enjoying our digital era, are giving our attention to technology for far more than just being able to enjoy convenience. How has technology managed to captivate our attention and why have we continuously invested our hearts, souls, and money into this digital age? Well, in our world where technology means cutting-edge, transformative, and revolutionary, our society has made it a priority to be valuable competitors in the race to create countless successful innovations. We generate advancements in communication, transportation, media, professions, and virtually every aspect of our lives faster than you can call out "Alexa.." to fulfill your request. All of this has come together to make technology become our life's source code. You might be wondering– where and how did technology become the center of our lives? Well, let's turn our focus to the start of a digital metamorphosis: the COVID-19 Pandemic.

The Pandemic Pivot

Let's go back in time and picture ourselves at the beginning of the year 2020. What do you see? Back then, how well did you know your way around the digital world? How often did you find yourself plugged in online? Were you tech savvy, or did you consider yourself a little fish in the big pond of the technology realm?

Before the pandemic hit, technology was a lifestyle idolized for its potential to unlock limitless innovations and successes. Classrooms were gradually incorporating computers into daily lessons. Office spaces were still struggling with in-person meetings, trying to squeeze them into packed schedules and in-between other appointments. But, when we fast-forward to the pandemic, technology had a new meaning. In a world where face-to-face interactions were limited, technology was no longer a convenience. Our lives drastically changed and we found ourselves relying on technology as the only thing keeping us functioning everyday. Technology, while our savior, shifted our lives to being plugged in online all day long.

As a result, we had a new best friend: our screens. We woke up to them, spent the day with them, and knew everything about them. We became accustomed to a digital world filled with online interactions, but did the pandemic reshape our relationship with technology forever? At the end of the pandemic, many of us expected to go back to our "normal" way of life– but what was normal had changed.

With the digital transformation in 2020, "normal's" new face looked like technology still lingering in our everyday routines. As the first year of the pandemic came to an end, it was just the beginning for a new player in our digital arena: artificial intelligence. The pandemic served as a motivator for developers to excel in their innovative creations, leading to the start of A.I. being used in our lives frequently. The pandemic forced us to be limited to our computers, so why not expand their capabilities and develop A.I. to be able to help us in more ways? At the time, many of us wondered, "Well, how can A.I. help us?"

Mind Bytes: Exploring the Rise of AI Thinking

Futuristic Sci-Fi movies introduced the world of Artificial Intelligence to us, often in the form of villain-themed thrillers or eutopia-themed stories that made us wonder what the future was capable of. Now, the future is here, and we no longer have to rely on two-hour long films to show us what impact AI has in our lives. To understand where AI is used in our lives, all we need to do is look everywhere– and I mean *everywhere!*

A.I. is not just limited to an office space or being used solely in a technology-driven lifestyle. Creations from A.I are used in our everyday lives, and are useful for all our different types of lifestyles.

Mapping and location, voice-assisted smartphones, handwriting recognition, language translation, and so much more took off in 2020 and guided us in advancements that continue to grow today. As the abilities that A.I have continue to grow, it is able to affect more areas of our lives and allow us to experience greater development made since 2020. Naturally, so many creations in AI, some that seem impossible to wrap our heads around, raise questions in all of us. How much influence does AI have in our lives? Will our world change for the better with this technology? What can we do now that you were not able to do before, thanks to A.I.?

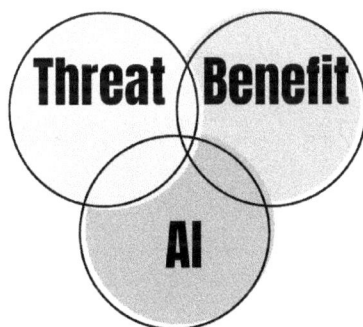

To understand the depth in the impact technology has had on our lives, let's explore in the following chapters each of our different social relationships, professions, education, and well-being. When forming our opinions on our new digital era, we will decode threat from benefit in the realm of technology, and explore what the future may have in store for us as we continue down the path of tech-evolution.

Chapter 2:

Our Life's Source Code: Technology

Technology once started as a tool for progress, crafted for our own benefit. Today, we have experienced how much technology has evolved as it has woven its way into our entire existence. Our digital age has reshaped how we interact, love, work, learn, and care for our well-being. As we try to navigate through unprecedented technological evolution, it is important for us to reflect on just how much we rely on technology, and in what areas of our lives technology lives.

Love, in all of its forms, is no longer limited to traditional face-to-face interactions. Traditional office spaces no longer rely on brick and concrete buildings, but instead thrive off of virtual connectivity. Our passions for knowledge and learning have reached far more people than ever before, with far more access to information than we've ever had. Our well-being and health have us feeling empowered and in charge of our own bodies with the help of technology and the growing wealth of research, medicine, and care it has given us. In these next chapters, let's explore in detail how technology has impacted us every day and minute of our lives.

Love, in all of its forms, is no longer limited to traditional face-to-face interactions. Traditional office spaces no longer rely on brick and concrete buildings, but instead thrive off of virtual connectivity. Our passions for knowledge and learning have reached far more people than ever before, with far more access to information than we've ever had. Our well-being and health have us feeling empowered and in charge of our own bodies with the help of technology and the growing wealth of research, medicine, and care it has given us. In these next chapters, let's explore in detail how technology has impacted us every day and minute of our lives.

Bits, Bots, and Beast: The Good the Bad and the Ugly of social emotional technology

Chapter 3:

Social Relationships in the Age of Screens

Logging On and Staying Connected

Online interactions are the first gateway to our growing digital era. Meetings, messaging, video chats, FaceTime – these are tools that have become essential to our daily existence. Think about it – how often do you find yourself benefiting from technological progress made in your life? We are constantly able to interact and stay up-to-date with each other despite distance and time differences. Staying connected over different parts of the world has become just as easy as clicking the "start meeting" button on any app on your phone or computer. Friends and family members are no longer limited to just Thanksgiving or holiday season visits with us as their only way of being present in our lives.

Maintaining connections with friends and family is just the beginning of online interactions. Creating new connections has become easier than we could have imagined by plugging in online. With just a few clicks we can create accounts that allow us to meet millions of new people, whether in our neighborhood or from across the globe, the possibilities are limitless. Bonding over common hobbies, interests, or skills based on our age, location, or experience has become easy with the ability to locate millions of more people through the internet. With new creations from A.I., you can even talk to an imaginary friend! Similar to how you are connecting with a real person online, you can create conversations and spend time with an A.I.-constructed friend.

Warning: Digital Disconnection Detected

How do you think these human and AI connections will turn out for us in the future? We are faced with a paradox of human versus online connection: do these online and AI connections truly fill the void, or do they sometimes leave us feeling lonelier when the screen turns off? Imagine you're staring at a screen, laughing, being excited, enjoying all of the conversation you are having with your companion over the phone, yet… you can't help but feel a partial emptiness as you log off or hang up from the conversation. It makes you stop and wonder– are these digital connections we are making real? Or are we becoming attached more to the pixels in our screens? In this new era of AI where we turn to technology for answers, advice, and conversation, the line between real and artificial interactions is more of a blur than ever before. Does the chatbot assisting us really care about the problem we have? Does the AI-inspired therapist truly understand our turmoil and emotions?

The Cold Embrace of Technology

We can agree that technology acts as a pathway to connect all of us together, but we are unable to get around the barrier it creates between us too. Sometimes, the screen is nothing more than a wall between us and the ones we bond with. With online interactions, we have the ability to avoid in-person encounters that demand a response in the moment. This barrier creates a space where we enjoy the comfort of being able to take our time to respond to messages, answer phone calls whenever we want, and enjoy the luxury of picking when we want to engage with others. But, what does this mean for the long-lasting connections we create online? A future concern is looming over our digital horizon– will we become so comfortable on our screens that our ability to create meaningful in-person interactions will suffer. It is only natural for us to question if all the feelings, emotions, and thoughts invested in online relationships will be transferred over to in-person connection, especially as we continue to rely more and more on digital communication.

While technology creates more connections for us online, it cannot create the one thing we rely on to create a genuine bond with one another– the hormone oxytocin. Oxytocin is a hormone that is connected with our trust and relationship building with others. The warm hug we need and the physical connection we long for ignites this love hormone we need to create meaningful relationships. If we need oxytocin so much, what happens when technology deprives us from it? When we lack oxytocin, we also lack emotional bonds and empathy, and instead we are left with an increased amount of stress. What does this mean for our future generations trying to form relationships? Are we seeing a generation of people forming that won't know the importance of a hug? Will they not understand the importance of physical connection?

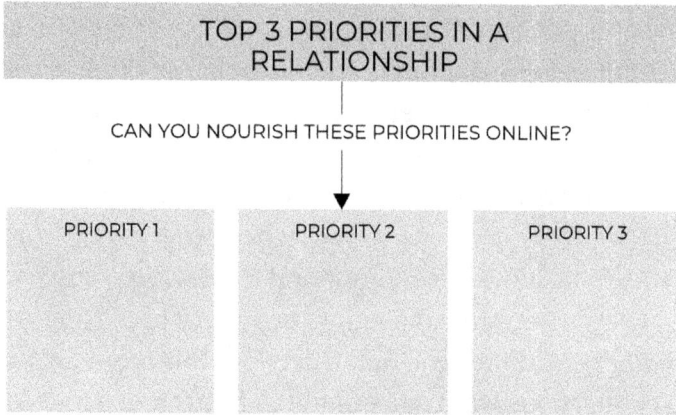

TOP 3 PRIORITIES IN A
RELATIONSHIP

CAN YOU NOURISH THESE PRIORITIES ONLINE?

PRIORITY 1   PRIORITY 2   PRIORITY 3

Chapter 4:

Finding Your Heart Online

Love Connecting Online

Back before technology became one of our closest, most reliable digital companions, people met their love interests through friend groups, school, work, or even the rare "randomly bumped into each other" romanticized scenario. But now, with the help of technology, our social circles have opened up to include more ways and chances we have in meeting our next love interest.

In this fast-paced digital realm of connections, many of us have also found that our love stories are online now. In the hustle and bustle of our everyday lives, who has the time to meet someone and make a romantic connection effortlessly?

This is where dating apps come into the arena of capturing our attention. With a variety of dating apps available at your fingertips, making romantic connections online has become a matter of convenience, ideal for fitting into our busy schedules. Imagine the euphoric feeling when stumbling upon your next love interest– these chances just soared in your favor. Whether looking for companionship or a deep love connection, technology has become our digital match-maker.

Finding romance online does not always mean using a conventional dating app now. The experience of meeting someone online and starting a relationship has shifted to include a variety of social media apps. All it takes to meet someone new is sending a direct message. With our social circles and ways to find love expanding, how has this affected the way we meet, think about, and interact with others?

Relationship Status: Heartbreak

It is an incredible advantage to have more possibilities of meeting new partners, but is it worth it having the negative effects of a swipe culture in our romantic desires? The swipe mentality describes a mindset influenced by the quick, often superficial decision-making associated with swipe-based mobile apps, which can impact how people approach dating, relationships, or other social interactions. The dark side of swipe culture revolves around the swiping mentality we adopt when meeting new prospect partners or other individuals. The swipe mentality is our quick, often superficial decision-making and judgment, physically swiping or even swiping only in our thoughts. This mentality affects our satisfaction in others, our genuine interest in them, and the amount of attention we give others becomes limited. Our attitudes and expectations are shifting from open-minded to quick judgment.

Have you ever swiped? Have you ever experienced the swiping mentality? Which side have you been on? Can you imagine finally gaining the courage to introduce yourself to your perfect crush, and feeling immediate heartbreak once you realize they are already judging your appearance before they even get to know you! Or, have you found yourself playing the role of someone who is quick to judge? Either way, an unavoidable consequence of a swiping mentality is the growing impatience and shortened attention span we give to others, hoping the next swipe will bring the perfect one. This cycle of swiping traps us in the illusion that our soulmates are right around the corner, but how do we know we haven't already swiped past them? That leaves us feeling empty and even more lonely.

Future Love Virus

Dating apps, social media apps, and other programs encourage our brains to be programmed to make rapid judgments, so even if we long for a deep connection with someone, how likely are we to set ourselves up for success? Our future may hold so many more options for love interests, but will we stay on the surface of finding love? People are more than just a couple of pictures, yet we only give them 30 seconds to make an impression. Do you think that's fair? What if someone treated you this way? Our next steps in our love story need to be acknowledging our tendency to swipe through potential connections. Our goal should be altering the swiping mentality mindset so we don't sabotage our opportunities for genuine connections with others in the future.

This digital tool paradoxically encourages people not to be honest and vulnerable, as they may lie about their age or enhance their photos to create a relationship which is inauthentic to begin with. We see this when people use catfishing to find new relationships, sometimes even long-term relationships. Catfishing is when someone uses a fake identity to communicate and create relationships with others. Some people catfish because they think they can only find love if they are someone else, oftentimes someone "better" than their real identity. One downside of this is people's self-esteem lowers from swiping, and trust is shattered when they don't really know the other person they are bonding with. Can we trust the person on the other side of the screen?

Chapter 5:

The Digital Boost in Our Professions

Proficiency Programmed in Professions

T echnology is not just a tool, it's the driving force behind a revolution in how we work and live, the source behind efficiency and productivity. Have you noticed yourself working differently? Is it faster, or even improved, as technology improves? Imagine all the tasks and responsibilities that would eat away at your time, that you can now resolve in mere minutes due to the power of technology. Whether you're crunching numbers, drafting reports, or designing masterpieces, the new digital revolution is there for you to rely on when reducing your daily To-Do lists. Job postings in newspapers have turned to listings on Craigslist, LinkedIn, and Indeed. These websites get us connected and help us stay up-to-date with employers, especially during the anxiety-filled interviewing process. Not only has this digital transition improved connections for employment, but employers have been able to find many more candidates than before, expanding beyond their neighborhood applicants to applicants across the world.

Our technological-ally does not stop at improving efficiency and productivity– it also expands into the realm of collaboration. Connections have become instantaneous, allowing your ideas, brainstorming, and creativity to be shared without having to go through countless phone calls and emails.

How do we collaborate now? Let's change gears and discuss why virtual meetings have become second-nature in our professional world. Have you ever needed to be in multiple places at once? The dread of commuting to a physical location is overwhelming, but now we have the ability to be anywhere we want with just a few clicks to join a virtual meeting. Virtual connections are becoming the norm as more workplaces offer hybrid and remote options. Getting rid of the traditional office space and converting to virtual saves money on rent, creates a convenience of working from home, and allows companies to be inclusive of so many more people who can aid their success from across the world.

Being in two places at once was once a dream, but has now turned to reality all while being able to do this from our own home. Virtual meetings are convenient, easy to create, and seamlessly allow collaboration to flow with minimal disruptions. We no longer have to travel to and from work, but instead we are now able to travel from our desk. Do you travel to work or do you travel from your desk? How did the virtual boost these past few years affect your work and professions?

BEFORE and AFTER

BEFORE

What were some limitations you experienced before technological advancements like video meetings, chatrooms, etc?

AFTER

What was made easier after these technological advancements were made?

Virtually Frustrated

On the flip-side, our reliance on technology in our professions has also caused frustrations, complications, and the occasional overwhelming feeling. Bring to mind your last virtual meeting, it took weeks to schedule and get everyone to log on together for 30 minutes. You are finally getting in the problem-solving flow your team desperately needs to move forward in your company goals— then a black screen instantly appears. Your computer died in just seconds, throwing off your entire creative flow and kicking you out of the meeting.

"How long does this take to charge?!" You yell out in frustration.

It could take several minutes for you to finally get back to the meeting– and then you have to play catch-up on all that happened while you were gone! While virtual communication is undeniably convenient, that does not erase the fact that many ideas and intentions can get lost in translation. We hit our heads against the keyboard when we think about how easy it would be to just *tell* someone in person what we think instead of writing a 10-paragraph email. We roll our eyes when placed on hold for a conversation that would take just 5 minutes if we could talk in person.

Another loss in the virtual professional industry is the loss of a cohesive personal in-person support system between you and your coworkers. How well would you say you know your coworkers in your remote world? The superficial conversations and short answers we give out during virtual meetings are only surface-based interactions. Body language, sharing a laugh, or even extending an invite to grab lunch together disappears in the virtual realm. For a thriving work environment, it is crucial to understand how meaningful connections are created and how to foster them, so it becomes clear that the challenge we must face now has turned virtual.

The Erasure of Roles and Careers

The workplace dynamics are at risk of losing personal touch, a theme we have seen ingrained in the virtual era we find ourselves in. Imagine your career transitioning, if it hasn't already, to being increasingly more virtual. Having your work entirely scheduled and conducted online can bring a huge level of comfort, especially when you appreciate all of your work being organized and in one place. But, is all this comfort such a good thing? The price we pay for comfort could lead to us giving up the personal, hands-on experience that is valued so greatly in the professional world. Are you willing to pay this price?

While our opportunities in our professions have increased tremendously with the virtual world, we often forget that means other people's opportunities have too. Competition over virtual and remote work has become almost impossible to beat after the pandemic now that our competitors are all over the globe, not just in our neighborhoods. When we finally do find a position we qualify for, companies now use Applicant Tracking Systems to quickly filter through the resumes we worked hours on. We can have a disadvantage in a matter of seconds if we are missing certain keywords, eliminating the personal touch of the hiring process.

Not only are the chances of finding a career limited at the application process– but technology can put us at a disadvantage before we even get the chance to apply! Companies are now choosing to replace our jobs with AI– all for convenience and cutting the cost of employing an actual person. This new understanding of what odds are weighing against us makes us worry! How confident are you going into your next job search? Are you ready to tell your next employer the qualities you have that AI can't match?

Chapter 6:

Education.edu

The Excellence of E-Learning

Education in the digital age has opened our eyes to just how much technology can impact us, our futures, and what opportunities we dream of. First, let's explore the power behind online learning. With our education being accessible online, we are able to learn on our own time AND from anywhere across the globe. That opens up more learning opportunities, one can learn any interest, even art or cooking, even if the school is not next to their home. Education online has shattered the boundaries of the traditional learning we have known for so long, and has made our dream education just a few clicks away from our reach. The digital world has impacted education so greatly that many universities have closed their in-person locations and have turned to operating only online.

Breaking free from the commutes, time constraints, and conflicting schedules never felt so relieving. Our advancing technology era gave us the key to unlock the door to our dreams in education and presenting them as a reality right before us.

Not only is our education at our fingertips with technology, but so is information. Facts, figures, and opinions are all a click away. A few minutes of typing and you can find yourself discovering all new ideas from any type of thought you had. Our web browser became our new library, one that has all the information we need– and it's incredibly simple to locate. We've replaced trips to the library with trips to our desk and opening dictionaries to opening Google. Now, with A.I, we are able to find all of the information we need in one place, but how accurate is this information we find and use from A.I.?

We all know, however, our education is much more than finding information at a fast rate. Education also lies in our everyday communication and connections with others too. We no longer have to cram our connections with others into the time we spend in the classroom. With technology, we are able to connect, share, and create communities from wherever and whenever through online interactions. In our digital realm of education, we have been able to create endless possibilities in learning, connections, creations, and interactions all through our keyboards.

Challenges in the Virtual Classroom

What has your experience been in this new way of education? Many people learn differently, and at different paces. Do you prefer education in-person? Or has online education introduced new ways you can find yourself excelling? These questions are important to ask as we navigate through the benefits and downsides of online education. Some of us can relate to struggling to learn online effectively. The essence of learning and whether it can be learned through a screen brings into light the traditional education system that has been used for centuries. Online education does provide flexibility, but does flexibility replace our face-to-face interactions and collaboration with other students? Will we thrive with an undemanding schedule that is too flexible for our own good? Self-determined schedules often make it harder for us to stay disciplined and on top of our assignments, papers, and even tests.

Evaluating Experience vs. Convenience

When taking our education into our own hands through virtual learning, we begin to wonder about the quality of our virtual educational experience. Does our virtual experience fall short of our potential learning in-person? The future complexities of online are less likely to be failed internet connections, but more likely to be non-existent personal connections with our peers and professors.

What lies ahead for our hands-on professions and learning experiences? Imagine studying biology or nursing without having stepped into a lab room or a hospital! Would this be ethical for the patients or populations that are relying on accuracy and efficiency? There is an irreplaceable learning opportunity that in-person, hands-on, education gives to us, and it cannot just be copied and pasted onto a screen. So, just how much of our education should be online? Who gets to decide what can and cannot be learned online? Well, the answer lies in your particular field of interest itself. Fields that bring life to theories, require hands-on practice, and enhance your knowledge through real-life experience will demand your personal presence. The balance between virtual and in-person learning rely on boundaries that we set in place, but how many will we need to keep setting in place when technology doesn't plan to stop evolving?

Some of your human teachers have transformed to be AI, robot teachers, in video, audio or even the metaverse. Are we benefiting from having a non-biased experience through AI teaching, or are we losing the personal connection with our mentor? By learning from humans we also gain their own experience they developed and can now teach, instead of just learning in a one-dimensional approach from AI material.

Think about one of your role models, what have you learned from their personal experience that affected you for a lifetime? Something you would not be able to take with you if it would be from an artificial machine?

Chapter 7:

Wellness, Well-being, and the Web

Healthy on Screen

W ell-being and technology are not an oxymoron. You will be amazed to find out that they have given us a greater sense of empowerment and accessibility in the world of Healthcare. Well-being is not just the absence of illness, it's about being active in choices and a lifestyle that benefits you.

One area of our well-being that benefits from our attention is our physical health. Taking the time out of our days to schedule an appointment that will happen weeks or months from now seems seems like such a bother, especially when we think about having to take off work or cancel plans so we can drive all the way to the doctor's office, sit in a waiting room for a long time, and only be at the appointment for five minutes. But, to our relief, technology has given us a much more efficient and convenient solution to this hassle!

Making an appointment with a primary care or a specialist has become easier and accessible than ever. Many telehealth companies send you medical kits which can be connected to the computer to make the appointment easier and feel like they are in person. Thermometers, pulse readers, and even ear scopes to detect ear infections can all be sent to your home! The ability to do these appointments from your couch is easier, especially with young kids sick at home.

"I don't have time for a doctor's appointment today–I'll just reschedule for another time..." We're all guilty of putting our health to the side as other priorities in our life take center stage.

"I feel fine so I am fine" and such rationalizing statements are false excuses we use that only enable us to put our well-being aside.

Our well-being was once something we dreaded dealing with, or we thought of as only a luxury for people who had the means or the time to go to a meditation class, hire a therapist or a nutritionist, or even exercise. The digital revolution turned these classic excuses and realistic obstacles to put our health as priority. Accessible tools like apps, chats, online groups concentrating on lifestyle opened the gates to better awareness on how we can improve our well-being.

Technology helps us not only when we are sick, when it's too late and we need to seek medical help, but helps us take two steps backwards to before we are sick and prevent the disease. We can now maintain our well-being so we can be in charge of our health. We no longer only go to the doctor when it hurts, but we use creative tools to maintain well-being, which is one of the core Positive Psychology foundations. No more going to the doctor's when it is already too late, now we can be ahead of our sickness and be proactive in maintaining a healthy lifestyle to prevent sickness– and technology is the path to create this awareness and take preventive measures.

Apps help us intertwine prioritizing our well-being in our lives every day, so we are more in tune with our health! Tracking steps, monitoring sleep patterns, counting calories, chatting with a health giver, and even recording the different chemical levels in our bodies are some of the few new tools technology provides for us to be active participants in our health and making choices for our well-being.

What else is essential to our health? Well-being extends beyond physical health, and so does technology. Self care and balance have become incredibly accessible to us through technology. Meditation apps help you create your peace after your overwhelming day, calming apps guide you back from the anxiety that tried to hold onto you so tight, and sleeping apps help you meet your goals of the sleep schedule we all dream of– literally.

Our mental health has technology as its support, too, especially in protecting us from isolation. Connections with mental health professionals through telehealth appointments, virtual support systems, and limitless resources are available for all of us, and something we are able to use on our own time and at our own pace.

Turning Health to a Virus

Place yourself in this scenario: you are logging onto your Telehealth appointment to show your doctor an injury that happened over the weekend. You believe it's minor, so you were just scheduled for a virtual consultation. The difficulty of trying to show your swollen ankle, hurt shoulder, or injured back to the doctor makes the entire virtual appointment seem ineffective. The reassurance you were trying to get from your doctor backfired, and now it seems you'll have to go to an in-person appointment anyways– but now they can't fit you into the schedule until months from now. We really value face-to-face chats with our doctors– they are personable, effective, and get things done at a fast pace. So are we sacrificing this essential part of health by relying on virtual appointments?

Personal Care? Or Robo-Care?

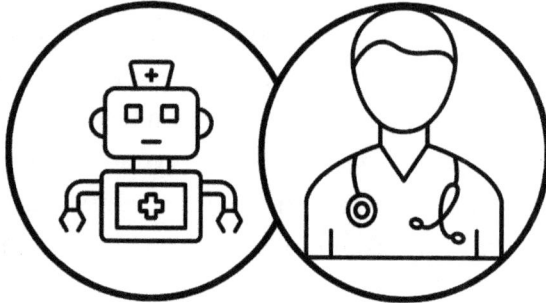

How deep are our connections with our doctors now that we are experienced with virtual appointments? When you log onto your appointment, do you feel you get the same care and attention as you would in-person? Online interactions can alter the way we view and treat others, including health professionals we feel disconnected from. On the other side of this daunting disconnection, how do you think the health professionals feel about us, their patients? When doctors are staring at a screen all day, it seems very likely they could feel that they are treating and caring for a screen, not real patients. Could this affect how doctors diagnose and influence an increase of misdiagnoses? Or even worse-could this potentially change how doctors practice medicine?

More therapists are working exclusively online for convenience and cost, but what does this cost us in healing? While we can connect to more therapists from across the world, do we lose the connection to nature, the best healer in the world? As human beings, our connection to nature will never be matched with a screen or keyboard. Feeling the warm sun beams, walking on grass, stretching in the cool breeze of fall are all natural healers our bodies rely on to stay happy and healthy. So, where does this happiness and healthiness go when we are glued to our screens everyday, paradoxically even in our mental health care.

Part C:

Hearts and Hardware: What is Emotional-Digital Literacy

Chapter 8:

What is Emotional-Digital Literacy?

D aniel, who is 36 years old, found out his girlfriend of 3 years was cheating on him. He is devastated and confused on what to do next, after he feels like his whole life has turned around. His time begins to only consist of sitting at home, blaming his ex-girlfriend for all that has happened. His anger begins to erupt more often, and he starts to take it out on others by yelling, having outbursts, and always listening to his negative thoughts. He begins to do things like overeat, get less sleep, and isolate himself from friends. His energy and focus shifts from taking care of himself to bombarding her with angry texts, non-stop calling her, and looking for ways to get revenge for all the hurt he feels.

He sits with his emotions without sorting through what intense feelings are coming from the amygdala as a stress response to the hurt. His brain is starting to be programmed to hyper-focus on the past and his future. Daniel's emotions are valid, but the way he faces them is only exacerbating the situation and the downfall of his well-being.

To get past his hurt, Daniel is in need of emotional skills and emotional knowledge to change his habits that come from hurt. Before we delve into what emotional-digital literacy is, let's discover what emotional literacy is. Let's examine what Daniel would do differently if he were to have emotional literacy skills.

Emotional literacy is understanding and managing your feelings and the feelings of others. Here are a few examples of practices which encourage emotional literacy:

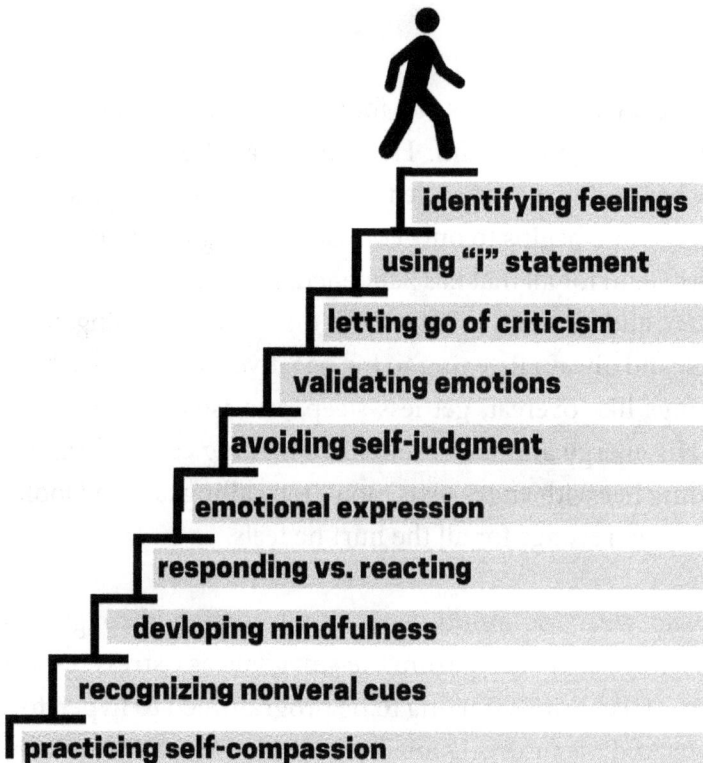

identifying feelings

using "i" statement

letting go of criticism

validating emotions

avoiding self-judgment

emotional expression

responding vs. reacting

devloping mindfulness

recognizing nonveral cues

practicing self-compassion

Now imagine that Daniel found his girlfriend cheating online, let's say through Instagram DMs. The emotions that Daniel feels become more complicated when his hurt is coming from a screen. Daniel doesn't know this other person on the screen, he only knows the pictures, likes, comments, and messages from this person that has contributed to so much hurt and changes in his life. He can't yell at the screen and feel better, it doesn't get through to the other person cheating. Is he messaging the other cheater, or does he feel more emptiness trying to convey his hurt through a keyboard? He is obsessing into finding more information about them, falling through of comments online, and relentlessly bashing the cheater's name online. He finds himself stalking all of this cheater's followers, and is now on track to become fully engulfed in his stalking behavior. Worst of all, Daniel starts bullying his girlfriend and every person he views as a contributor to his hurt. He posts about himself on his social media, alluding to an eventful, fun, and busy life when in reality he is feeling empty. His emptiness is magnified when he becomes trapped in a loop comparing himself to others.

Most people have difficulties identifying their emotions and feelings when they are in stress or a hard situation, let alone managing with them. Think how complicated it is to deal with these emotions when we are adding the complex unknown digital realm.

How can the emotional and digital world overlap without us falling apart from our overwhelming emotions? This is where the concept of emotional digital literacy comes into play, equipping us with valuable tools that benefit our emotional healing.

What does emotional digital literacy mean for us? It is our heightened self-awareness and understanding of what responses are triggered by technology and the knowledge of how to cope after these triggers have affected us. We can think of emotional digital literacy as a mirror that lets us reflect on how technology impacts our lives since we constantly interact with it. This mirror helps us see our own responses, emotions, thought processes, and problem-solving skills, while also giving us insight into new tools that help us harness our emotional literacy.

The psychological and the emotional dynamic between us, human beings, and the digital realm is not clear-cut. There are many complexities that arise when we, living human beings, interact with artificial developments like technology. We are so distracted by technology in our daily lives that we overlook a vital part in the world of digital: our role. When we come into the picture, we see how technology is not just a tool that we can use and discard when we choose, but that it also does something much more influential. Technology can influence our emotions, shape our identity, and change the way our brains are programmed to understand, react, and interact with one another. How can we manage to handle all of this power that technology holds? We can start by equipping ourselves with the tools from a new concept in our digital era: emotional digital literacy.

Can you imagine if Daniel had a solid understanding of emotional literacy skills and developed emotional intelligence from a young age? How would that affect him? How would that affect recovery from the breakdown of his emotions? How does that affect not only him, but everyone around him?

The 8 Tools of Emotional Digital Literacy

After in-depth research and careful case analysis, I have determined that there are eight primary tools in emotional digital literacy:

Let's examine the essential tools of emotional digital literacy:
1. **Assessing self-awareness**
2. **Regulating emotions**
3. **Applying critical thinking**
4. **Creating digital boundaries**
5. **Navigating digital citizenship**
6. **Staying in the present**
7. **Fostering relationships in the digital era**
8. **Balancing lifestyles**

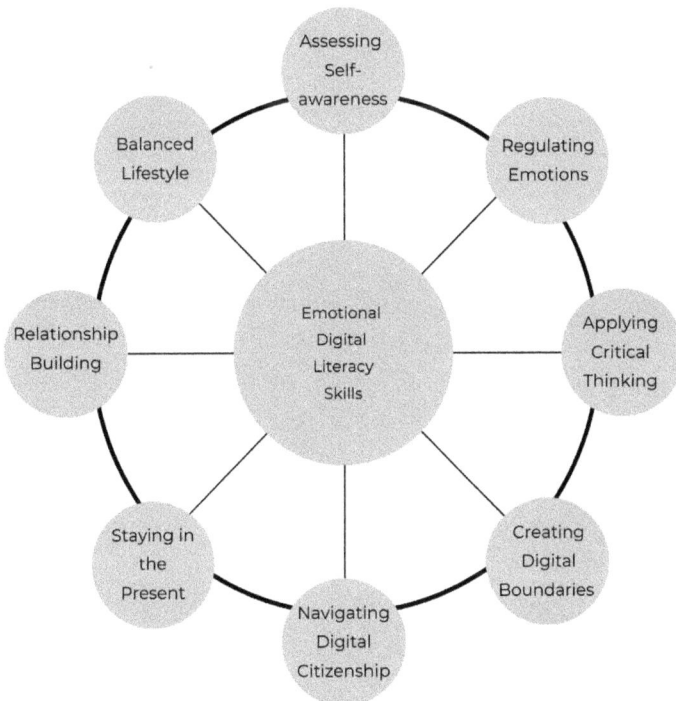

Through this ever-evolving change in technology, it is crucial for us to recognize our role, what value it has, and continue familiarizing ourselves with necessary tools to foster balanced engagement with technology. As long as technology continues to develop, our involvement in the digital era will continue to change and grow along with it. We can thrive in this process of creating a healthy, balanced lifestyle by learning about what emotional digital literacy can provide for us in these next chapters.

Chapter 9:

Emotional Digital Literacy Tool Box: Practicing Our New Strengths Everyday

1. Assessing Self-Awareness

After a long and busy day, all you want to do is lay down and unwind before you have to start your day all over again in what feels like just a few hours. You fix yourself a quick dinner, and without thinking too much about it, you pick up your phone and start scrolling through social media as a way to unwind, relax, or out of boredom, and take your mind off of what your responsibilities are tomorrow. You giggle and laugh as you watch a few funny videos— but your laughter comes to a halt as you stumble upon a video that you disagree with. You can feel a sense of strong emotions starting to arise. The next thing you know, you can't keep yourself contained and you start commenting on the post. Now, you added a few accounts which are not considered as friends, but as components who you will be waiting for their raging response. You lash out with harsh words, arguing with others in the comments section. Scrolling was supposed to help you calm down and fall asleep, but has quickly turned to your blood pressure and adrenaline rising and keeping you on high alert.

These reflective questions are the foundation for assessing our self-awareness in our digital realm. Assessing our self-awareness includes understanding and recognizing our emotional responses to digital content and online interactions that we engage with every day.

Before we let our emotions consume us and motivate our actions, we need to pause and ask ourselves:

What emotions does this media content trigger for me?
What emotions do I get from engaging with others online at this moment?

Examining the "why" is also an important contributor to self-awareness because it helps us reflect on the cause of our strong emotions, and what to expect the next time we stumble upon content that is similar to what triggered us the first time. What is it about that post or online interaction that triggered such intense feelings? Did the digital content negatively impact personal experiences, beliefs, or insecurities? By asking these questions, we not only see the root of our emotional reactions, but also can reflect on our own morals and values.

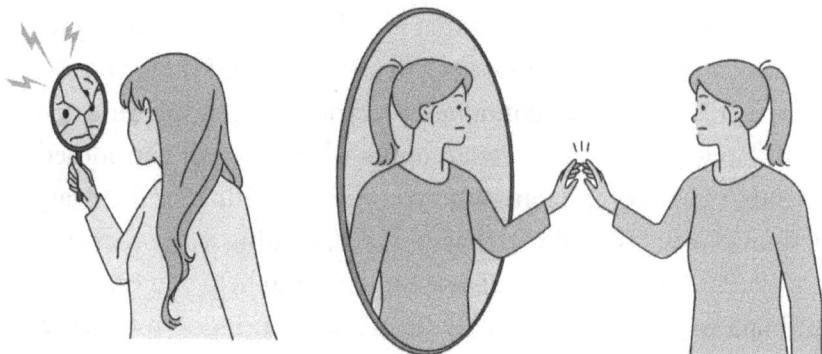

Steps to Assess Your Self-Awareness

How do we make sure we are assessing our self-awareness? Here are the key guiding steps to follow:

1. **Keep an eye on digital consumption:** It is important to pay attention to how much time you spend online, what content you engage with, and what type of media you tend to always watch. By monitoring these three things, we can remind ourselves when we should step away from our screens, redirect ourselves to look at different content, or notice specific themes or topics in content that trigger us.

2. **Self-reflect on and off the screen:** Emotions can get the best of us, and cause immediate reactions we later regret. As a final step in self-awareness, it is important to ask yourself: How would I respond to the comments I am making online? How would I feel if someone acted the way I am acting? Do I project negativity or positivity? In doing so, we not only realize the impact our actions have on others, but we can also assess if our reactions are conveying what we actually mean and feel.

3. **Intentions on the internet:** When engaging online with others or with media, think about this: What are my Intentions? Despite what our intentions may be, our actions do not always match them. Because of this, it's important to make sure we reflect on what we actually want to accomplish. What are your intentions? Do you wish to make friends? Win an argument? Make a difference? Get attention you don't usually get? Influence others? Educate? Brag? Think about what you are posting and why.

Unveiling our self-awareness is the pause that we need amongst overwhelming emotions that can tower over us. Using these steps going forward can change our online experience to be more intentional and meaningful by taking out the impulse that can get the best of us.

2. Emotional Regulation

Alex is in the middle of midterms at his university, and is feeling extremely overwhelmed with studying and completing assignments that are due in one week. With this tight deadline, he feels he has so much on his plate, almost like it's impossible to get his work done on time. As he is finishing another study guide for one of his classes, he gets an email from one of his TAs that he is missing an assignment, and if he wants full credit he will have to turn it in by the end of the day.

With this new addition to his To-Do list, Alex feels like his anxiety is going to burst through his chest. His face scrunches with anger, and he can feel his eyes starting to water as a wave of emotions drown out his voice of reason. His initial reaction is to shut down and even email his TA telling them he won't be able to complete the assignment. But, instead of letting negativity overpower him, he reminds himself of how to use emotional regulation to reset his emotions and mind instead of firing off a heated response.

When you feel triggered by technology or social media, effective strategies to calm your emotional storm is essential to keeping a balanced lifestyle with digital content, and is the foundation of regulating your emotions. The digital realm can trigger a wide range of emotions, including anger, sadness, and anxiety. Sometimes, we can even find ourselves shutting down from being overwhelmed by these feelings. When we find ourselves in this position, we can reflect on these strategies to ensure our emotions do not trigger actions before we have a chance to think about them.

While recognizing your emotions is the first step, the second step is knowing how to calm yourself down. You can follow these strategies to de-escalate from your intense feelings on the screen.

How to Handle Your Emotional Rollercoaster

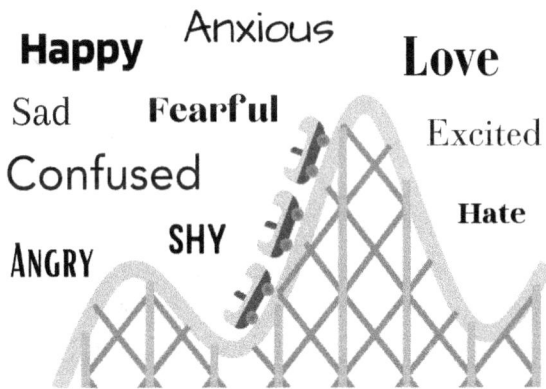

Happy Anxious **Love**

Sad **Fearful** Excited

Confused

Hate

ANGRY SHY

1. **Pause the screen and pause the mind:** When you begin to feel intense emotions arise, take a moment to step away from your screen and reflect on what you are feeling, and why you might be feeling this way.

2. **Recognize digital triggers:** Once you start to familiarize yourself with your digital triggers, you can set up digital boundaries that will prevent you from being overwhelmed with intense emotions. Ask yourself what is your trigger? Email notifications? Political posts by others? Endless search on shopping apps? Constant phone calls and texting

throughout the day? Know you have choices. You can disable the notification which creates the trigger. Maybe utilize your "do not disturb" function on your phone when you need to concentrate and not be distracted. Unfollow accounts that leave you feeling drained, anxious, or angered constantly. Ultimately, limit your access to multiple media outlets that are trying to get your attention all at once. By allocating specific time for certain media content to reach you, you can avoid being overwhelmed from your devices.

3. **Reboot and return:** One of the most difficult parts of managing your emotions is when you are responding to what is triggering you. It is very simple to hit send once you've unleashed all of your intense emotions that were evoked in a few split seconds, but that does not mean it is beneficial. Before you hit the send button, make sure you have taken your time in communicating what you mean, how you feel, and what outcome you are looking for. Write out a response, but wait a few minutes before you send it. Look over your reply a few times to make sure your emotions aren't taking full control and overpowering what you truly mean.

Although Alex is struggling with being overwhelmed, he takes a moment to back away from the screen in front of him. He recognizes the digital triggers that overwhelm him, and make him feel like he has enough time to even finish his assignments. He refocuses his attention to the assignments that are due first, and silences his apps on his phone and computer so he won't be distracted or have to worry about other things taking his focus away. Once he uses his "do not disturb" and silences his notifications, Alex felt a relief, he maximized his time to complete his assignment. By 5pm he completed his assignment. Instead of sending his TA an angry email, or even asking for an extension, his self esteem and confidence rises - Alex did it, all by himself! (He received A- on his assignment).

In the digital age, our emotional rollercoaster often accelerates as we interact with technology. The strategies that Alex has followed is the essence of managing your emotions online, an essential skill that often escapes us as being necessary. Regulating your emotions is a skill that grows stronger over time, so it is important to keep practicing and be mindful when experiencing new emotions, responses, and circumstances you encounter.

3. Critical Thinking

We usually associate critical thinking with education, research, and problem-solving in our lives, but should technology and media be considered too? Does social media come to mind when you think about critical thinking? How can we use critical thinking to guide us in our relationship with technology?

Harper, a devoted dancer, is starting to struggle with her body image. Her friends in her dance program are all starting to look thinner than her, which brings up insecurities for Harper when they're practicing and performing together. To make things worse, when Harper scrolls through her social media, she sees countless accounts of young adults like her, who are thin and beautiful. What her mind neglects to remember, is that most of them, if not all, are photoshopping their photos and bodies to make themselves look thinner. She feels horrible about herself.

As she is trapped in this cycle of comparing herself to social media posts, she stumbles on an advertisement for a weight loss supplement. There is an illusion of hope. She spends her next few minutes scrolling through review videos for this brand, seeing beautiful people excitedly tell her in 10 seconds why the supplement is the "best" one. Harper skims over a few comments, glances at a couple of reviews, and is adding the supplement to her online shopping cart all within just a few minutes of seeing the original post advertising it.

In this rush of excitement and hopes to quickly solve her insecurity, Harper neglects to use critical thinking when interacting online. Without critical thinking, she didn't stop to ask herself:

"Did I see enough evidence that shows this supplement truly works?"
"Can I prove this is even healthy for me?"
"Do I even need this supplement?"

Critical thinking is evaluating digital content, information, and interactions with a discerning and thoughtful mindset. When using critical thinking, we help protect our overall well-being, including our mind, body, and emotions.

Instead of being so quick to decide on buying a supplement in efforts to solve her insecurity, Harper could work on solving the puzzle within digital content by being more careful and diligent with new information. With critical thinking Harper would find out that the ad spotted her emotional fragile moment. The desire to be better, prettier, thinner played a major role in her decision making, skipping the most important part - processing the decision making and how it is realistically can affect her life. Harper can use critical thinking by using multiple trusted sources, taking time to reflect on her *own* thinking uninfluenced by others, and collaborating with others that have used the supplement to help form a well-rounded opinion.

Here is the critical thinking process Harper would benefit from when interacting online:

Critical Thinking Process

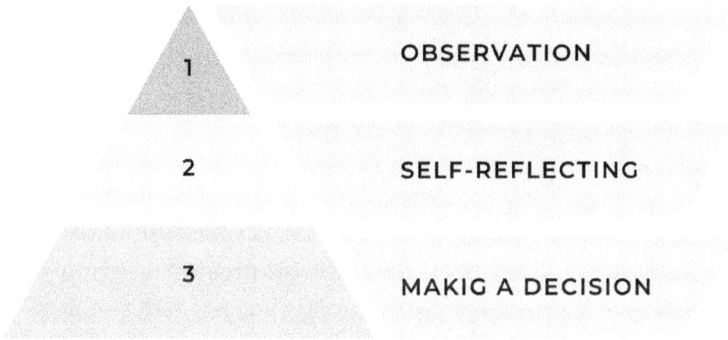

1 OBSERVATION

2 SELF-REFLECTING

3 MAKIG A DECISION

1. **Observation:** Integrate multiple sources and perspectives when interacting online. When you limit yourself to one source, you are limiting your own knowledge. It is important to seek depth and a broad scope of perspectives with digital content.

2. **Self-reflecting:** Reflecting on our own learning and thinking is crucial when using digital content, especially since we are constantly fed opinions and perspectives from others. Take the time to separate the thoughts you come up with yourself from the thoughts that were given to you. By doing this, we can listen to our own mind and intuition when faced with decisions, when giving feedback, or when providing input.

3. **Making a decision:** Once you've developed your own opinion, take a moment to pause. At times, the key lies in allowing room for a deliberate decision. If you find

yourself still perplexed, seeking guidance from a trusted individual, such as a mentor or an objective guide is valuable. Recognize that decision-making is a process that involves distinguishing emotions from intuition, understanding the two components at play

Before hitting the "buy" button, Harper stopped and stared at her screen. She felt uncertain, and whenever she felt this way she knew she could always go to her dancing coach for advice. They have known each other for years and had created a strong sense of trust with each other. Harper knew there was nobody better to go to for some help.

Harper confessed all her feelings and insecurities that had come up recently whenever she came to dance. It felt like a weight had been lifted off of her chest. After confiding in her coach, she realized that in a moment of overwhelmed emotions she was jumping into a decision that was based on comparing her inside to other's outside. Not thought out carefully, she almost risked her well-being for a supplement that promised her a perfect-ideal-illusionary body, with ingredients she knew little about. Because of her use of the critical thinking process, Harper did not end up using the supplement to quickly fix her insecurity. She also became encouraged from the critical thinking process to help her fellow dancer friends that also struggled with body image, and created the balanced environment their well-being could thrive in.

4. Digital Boundaries

Ryan is a 30-year-old teacher who is very passionate about keeping up-to-date with current events. His interests include politics, social media, and socializing with his fellow teaching friends and his family in his spare time. His social circle grows every day, as he is very outgoing and loves meeting new people. Ryan's outgoing personality contributes to how well-spoken he has become, especially with his experience as a teacher, which helps him tremendously when he is expressing his thoughts and opinions to others. One way Ryan does this is through Twitter, where he posts multiple times a day for his hundreds of followers to see.

Tweeting and replying to comments all day long is a normal habit Ryan has adopted, but he doesn't realize how draining it is becoming for him. *Bing! Bing! Bing!* His phone buzzes all day long with Twitter notifications, triggering the urge to respond to every comment he receives. It disrupts the flow of his day, peace of mind not to mention how it is interfering with meetings and conversations he has in person with others. He can't help but to glance at his phone to see what someone replied to his post.

"Do they agree with me?"
"How could they say something like that?"
"They are wrong! I need to show them why they're wrong..."

All of these thoughts pop into Ryan's mind when he hears his phone go off, making him completely separate himself from what's actually happening in real life. He becomes fixated on comments he disagrees with, and always has to make sure he points out when he thinks someone is wrong, out of line, or something he just disagrees with.

What was once a simple debate and matter of opinion has turned to constant arguments, name-calling, shaming, and vulgar talk between him and another person behind a screen. Ryan has even extended beyond Twitter, and has created multiple online accounts across different media platforms so he can always stay in the loop and tell people his thoughts and opinions. He always feels defensive, even when he is not typing on his phone or looking at his social media accounts. Ryan's fight-or-flight and adrenaline rush he gets from constant arguments never really dwindles away, and this is starting to affect how he treats people face-to-face. He doesn't notice anymore when he raises his voice, interrupts others, or even when he stops listening altogether because he thinks he is only right.

Ryan's identity becomes who he presents himself as in social media. While Ryan's voice does matter, is the way he is expressing his thoughts and opinions benefiting his well-being and relationship with others? How can Ryan resolve his impulse to constantly engage with this negative online content?

To start, establishing and maintaining healthy limits on your technology usage will protect your emotional well-being. With this in mind, where should he draw the line when tweeting and commenting online?

Let's explore some ways on how to create digital boundaries.

Protecting Your Emotional Bliss

1. **Emotional investment boundary:** The emotions we invest into our interactions online often determine what interactions we can expect and how we will feel after. Are you investing a lot of anger into your arguments and conversations online? This could lead to feeling emotionally drained and uncertain about your decisions. Do you often feel you are experiencing sadness or anxiety when talking to others through a screen? These feelings can lead to affecting your confidence and esteem in future interactions. It is therefore important we are mindful of what emotions we are investing in on our screens and talking to others, and even more crucial to ask ourselves "How is this interaction benefiting me? Is it disturbing my peace of mind?"

2. **Emotional hula hoop:** Who are you interacting with online when you engage in conversations, arguments, or quick talks? Do you know these people online, or are they just an account with a profile picture on your screen? Who we let into our emotional hula hoop will affect your time investment online and what emotions are brought up when interacting with them. Do you know all your followers? When you don't even know the first name of the person you are arguing with online, is arguing with them worth the emotional toll it takes on you? Your emotions not only affect you but they affect others too. Your digital citizenship, or how you treat and speak to others online, is heavily influenced by your emotions. Out of anger, you made vulgar comments to someone you barely even know! Why are you choosing to let strangers enter into your emotional space?

3. **Time boundary:** Balance and time are two intertwined core foundations of a balanced lifestyle, and that includes our relationship with technology. How much time you choose to invest in interacting online with others will affect your mindset and attitude when communicating in real life or other online areas. Too much negativity consuming your life will alter your well-being and how you communicate when you aren't online. This is why it is essential that digital boundaries also include limitations online so that digital interactions do not take over your everyday interests, hobbies, or activities. A great way to ensure you are setting a time boundary with digital interactions is to set aside time to disconnect from it. Create routines that allow you to stay focused on your real-life interactions and experiences with others, free from your devices. It is very easy to get lost in time when you're scrolling on your screen. One minute turns into one hour, and within that hour your emotions and thoughts can disorient you from stepping away from the screen. When you find yourself giving time to digital devices, incorporate time to step away from your screen so you can focus on other hobbies, interests, or tasks that need your attention. Digital breaks allow you to regroup and come back to your screen with a fresh mind, and when you do come back to your screen make sure to utilize all the previous digital skills discussed so far.

What do I keep private? Do I respond to all these comments online I am getting? Do I copy and paste from Chat GTP? What pictures do I post for my online profile? Digital boundaries expand to all these areas of our world in technology, and are all related through being mindful of your emotions, space, and time you want to create for yourself. Creating boundaries you are comfortable with is the first step, then as more questions about the online world come up, you can decide based on these boundaries you created!

5. Digital Citizenship

Dakota is a dedicated and successful video gamer whose skill level can be measured by the hundreds of hours she spends online. With all this time logged on to her gaming console, Dakota is constantly interacting with other gamers, which has led to her feeling comfortable and valuing her gaming community and online friends.

After work, *PING!* Dakota logs onto her game. After dinner, *PING!* More of her time is spent playing video games. She texts her family that she has to cancel her weekend plans with them because she has to finish passing the last level on her game. Dakota entered a video game tournament at the end of this month, so she avoids making any other plans with family and friends so her full attention can belong to the game.

Dakota's time, interest, and emotional investments are all being given to her gaming without much thought because all she can think about is winning and unlocking new achievements. Her video game virtual world has become the only world she cares about, so she loses touch with her real life beyond technology. Becoming so comfortable with her virtual world, Dakota starts to lose touch on the difference between the virtual and real world. This affects how she starts treating her online friends as she starts to feel she is just talking to a screen and no longer talking to an actual person with real emotions and experiences.

Dakota's starting to argue more with her online friends, uses vulgar and inappropriate language without thinking about it, and is even being called a bully with her behavior targeting people in video game chats she hardly knows. Dakota starts to lose friends left and right, and more people hear about her hurtful behavior and start avoiding her. She often plays with one or two people now instead of big groups, and is heartbroken when her online friends tell her they no longer want to play online or be friends. Dakota's behavior is an example of a very common scenario: losing sight of digital citizenship.

Digital citizenship is the practice of responsible and ethical behavior online, including the consideration of how your behavior impacts others. How did Dakota's vulgar words affect her online friends? How did her bullying impact how others view her?

To stay in touch with digital citizenship, consider these three behaviors:

The Harmony of Digital Citizenship

1. **Responsible behavior:** Responsible behavior online is defined through thinking before you act and fostering a safe environment. Before you send your reply online, think about how this could impact someone you know, or even you only know through a screen. Do you know their circumstances? They might not respond or understand the way you anticipated. Feeling safe and comfortable online is also key to forming bonds with others through a screen, and safe environments are created through being open-minded to all people and embracing diversity. You can become a leader, and it is your responsibility to make choices on how you lead

others, your followers. Holding yourself accountable for these actions will promote community between you and the online community.

2. **Ethical behavior:** Ethical behavior means doing what is right and fair. It's about being honest, treating others with respect, and making good choices even when no one is watching. It's like following a set of rules or principles that help you be a good and responsible person. Ethical digital behavior is seen through respect, fairness, and values online. Respecting others that share the same digital space is one way ethical behavior is seen online. In any scenario, when you hope to create a friendship, belong to a community, or lead others. Respect can be shown through being considerate of people's privacy and also treating others how you would like to be treated. Do you appreciate vulgar language being thrown at you? Of course not! No one does. So when working with others it is important to remind yourself to allow space for your peers to express themselves in a healthy way. What are your values in real life? Are you still keeping them in digital space? If someone is crossing yours, are you still engaging with them? Do you value the way you are treating others or how people treat you?

3. **Empathetic behavior:** Empathy towards others is how relationships thrive, including online relationships. Your own circumstances are unique, and it's important to remember that this applies to everyone you meet online. Technology has allowed us to meet thousands of people from across the world, but as we meet new people, we need

to consider that the background people come from become more and more different. We do not know what the person behind the screen just went through. Our minds tend to create stories about people based on their past, traumas, and experiences, often jumping to conclusions from just their pictures or words. We rush to judge. Your experience online may be far greater than someone else. Are you talking to someone across the globe from a different culture? Do they understand your intentions or customs? Are they grieving a medical, financial, emotional loss or a breakup? Empathy can bridge the gap between different experiences and circumstances we encounter essential to digital citizenship.

YOUR GOAL
Digital Citizenship

STEP BY STEP CHECKLIST

- [ ] Think before you act

- [ ] Consider their circumstances

- [ ] Treat others with respect

- [ ] Allow others to express themselves

- [ ] Show others empathy

- [ ] Contribute to creating a safe online environment

After her teammates had an intervention with Dakota and expressed their frustrations and hurt caused by her behavior. They explained how her tendency to use vulgar language and bully scared off people from logging online with her anymore. Her online friends expressed they missed playing video games with Dakota, but unless she showed some effort in changing her behavior, they couldn't bring themselves to join her online anymore. After hearing how much her actions impacted others, Dakota made the decision to try and start using digital citizenship when she logs online so she can save her online friendships.

Imagine if people used digital citizenship when interacting with others online. Instead of the online world feeling threatening in situations where you are just trying to be yourself, online environments would be a safe place for you to express your thoughts, feelings, and opinions. Vulgar language in intense arguments would no longer box you into a corner because the use of digital citizenship would promote respect between you and other people online. Empathy and compassion for others promoted through digital citizenship will combat the bullying so commonly seen online, and replace this negativity with space for diversity.

As our lives continue to intertwine with more advanced technologies, like AI, digital citizenship is also important to use so we remain authentic and ethical in our own creations. For example, Chat GTP may be very useful when used as a guide, but digital citizenship draws a definitive line between using Chat GTP as a tool and plagiarizing. Ethical, responsible, and empathetic behavior is also crucial when considering how complex fraud and fake identities have become with the use of AI. The use of AI has made online fraud behavior harder to detect, trace, and control. Because of this, education on digital citizenship early will have a proactive effect on combating and limiting how many will be impacted by the negative side of the online realm.

6. Staying Present

Ping! Reuben picks up his phone without even thinking, as soon as he hears the sound go off. Another comment, another like for his TikTok account. *Ping! Ping!* He picks up his phone again, scrolling through the notifications just from one minute ago.

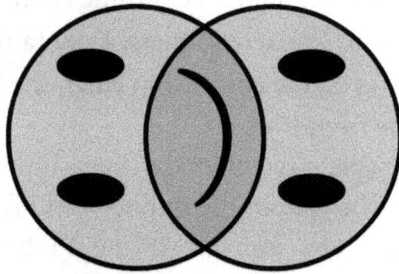

Reuben is *finally* spending quality time with his **girlfriend** after weeks of planning just a few hours that fit into both of their schedules. They are both relaxing at Rueben's apartment, watching their favorite dating show that just came out with a new episode. The two of them follow along with each character's love story, but Rueben loses his focus every time his phone buzzes. He doesn't remember some characters' names, and has no idea their backstory. His girlfriend makes a joke about one of the relationships on the show, but Reuben doesn't laugh because he doesn't get it. *Ping!* He checks his phone immediately, causing him to be further and further away from his present quality time with his girlfriend. Social media, emails, comments, all take up Rueben's attention, and he can't help but always look at his screen.

"Huh?" Reuben replies for the third time in a row, every time he isn't listening to what his girlfriend is trying to tell him. Reuben's girlfriend is feeling so frustrated and hurt from feeling so ignored, all because of a phone.

The compulse Reuben has to always be connected online has led him to mindlessly ignore all else around him whenever his phone demands for his attention. Not only is Reuben being inconsiderate of his girlfriend's time and feelings, but his mindlessness is making him become so disconnected that he doesn't realize when he looks away from reality and looks to his screen instead. This compulsive behavior from Reuben ultimately serves no real benefit to him, but does more harm as his brain is becoming hardwired to react to a ringtone.

After countless times of being ignored, Reuben's girlfriend gets up to leave early.

"I feel like your phone is more important than spending time with me, your girlfriend. You aren't engaging with me anymore, you're just engaging with your screen," Reuben's girlfriend explains.

After hearing this, Reuben feels terrible. Of course he wants to spend time with his girlfriend, but he can't help but look at his phone. It feels like just seconds he's looking at his screen but those seconds are long minutes in reality. How can Reuben keep from acting compulsively and mindlessly? How can Reuben show his girlfriend he values their friendship more than his phone?

Mindful engagement with technology is intentional and with awareness of your actions and thoughts while online, rather than giving into impulses or mindlessness. When using technology, there is a time and a place where online engagement will not impose on your environment or on others. How do we know when is the right time to be online?

Here are three suggested guidelines to use for mindful engagement with technology:

The Mind Online and Offline

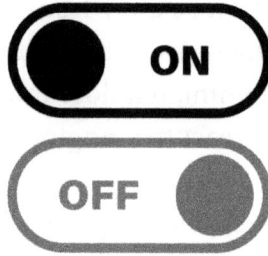

1. **Is this the time or place for technology?** Online engagement has become so accessible to us anytime of the day or night with our phones, computers, and many more devices that are convenient. With this, however, comes the new expectation that we are always reachable and ready to connect. Not only does this encourage us to mindlessly and compulsively always check our messages, posts, or emails, but it also creates a mindset that prioritizes devices over our present. Ask yourself if answering your phone can be done at some other time that won't take away from your present time. Can I answer the message later today? Can this post wait until tomorrow? Can my reply to this email wait until Monday when I am back at work?

2. **Prioritizing the present:** there is a very common illusion that social media creates: the illusion that you are missing out when you are not online. This is what keeps dragging us back to constantly be invested in our screens. What are my

friends doing? What is the latest gossip? Who is online right now? What are the latest trends? All of these concepts take us away from what we are actually missing out on– the present. When we are so worried about missing out online, we miss out on the real connections instead. The person in front of you, the reality you are in right now but ignoring for a screen, are what's real. To replace this online illusion, the use of mindfulness can keep you grounded and focused on the present so you can stay up-to-date with what really matters.

3. **Build digital resilience:** Whenever we practice a new skill, like mindful engagement, there can be setbacks that may feel discouraging. You heard your social media notification sound three times in a row, and even though you're at an important dinner you can't help but check it. Being able to bounce back from setbacks will make your resilience stronger, especially when you come across new challenges. You may have checked your phone, scrolled through your social media when you wish you hadn't, but reminding yourself to be mindful and being reflective on what you can do better in the future will build you up for success.

To show his girlfriend how important he is, Reuben knows he needs to change his attitude regarding the time and energy he invests in his constant need to respond and get updated. He commits to put down his phone and practices mindfulness instead of staring at his screen. The instagram posts he was liking will be there tomorrow, the text messages will still show up on his phone later, and the email responses could wait until the weekend is over, but putting his best friend on hold while he answered the rest of the world was no longer going to be Reuben's mindset. It isn't easy, but Reuben looks for replacements so he can focus better on the present time and people in his life. Slowly, this process creates a stronger sense of value between Reuben and his girlfriend, making his girlfriend feel like a valued person is his life. This echoes back to Reuben, making him feel valued and prioritized in his relationship too.

7. Relationship Building

Natalia is a very shy person who enjoys her personal alone time and quiet hobbies that help her stay relaxed. Her nights usually consist of working on her latest digital artwork and posting it to her social media art account that she has spent a long time building her one thousand follower fan base. She applied for a position to work at a smoothie bar on the weekends to realize she has a more outgoing and confident side to her. She likes talking to new people. Since she started working, Natalia has made more friends and is starting to go out of her comfort zone to start conversations with people she meets.

Over a few months of making smoothies at her new job, Natalia starts to have a crush on one of the regular customers that comes in every weekend. She wants to talk to him, but every time she sees him she feels like she can't get words out. All she knows is his first name, even after months of seeing him come into the smoothie bar. Natalia can't help but wonder so much about him and just wants the opportunity to get to know him, but all she can manage to do is greet him and smile politely when he orders at the register.

One day when Natalia is working on her digital art, she logs onto her social media and posts her latest piece. Her crush from the smoothie bar never really leaves her mind, she keeps thinking about him and anticipates seeing him during the weekend. As she's scrolling through her screen, a thought pops into her head:

"I wonder if I can find out more about him on social media?"

Natalia starts typing to search his name and find out if she can stumble upon his own social media accounts. She spends the rest of her night squinting her eyes to see if the tiny profile picture matches the crush she eagerly looks for. It's way past the time she planned to go to sleep, but Natalia is still scrolling on her screen because she would rather be digitally connected with her crush from the smoothie bar than have to start a conversation with him in person. She finally finds the page she is looking for, and scrolls through his pictures and the people he knows (especially the females) all night without having said one word to her crush in person or online.

The next time Natalia sees her crush at work, she can't help but feel like she is hiding something. Natalia feels like she knows him, but she really only knows his social media account. She spent hours on her phone getting to know her crush's latest posts, comments, likes, but what does this translate to in real life? Natalia contemplates on creating a fake account so she can start talking with her crush freely. She even considers using AI to create fake pictures so she can hide behind a make-believe person. After all, they have a lot in common, they both like the same music, eating healthy and art. But, she still is unable to start a conversation with him and he walks out of the shop for the third time in a row without having a talk with Natalia.

Why would Natalia spend so much of her time online trying to find her crush's account? This is happening because she is focused on fostering her digital relationships to avoid creating meaningful connections in person where she feels more vulnerable and might get rejected. Online relationship is creating a space and walls between her heart and reality. But, is the time and effort invested digitally identical to what is needed in real life?

This is not only Natalia's story but a common trend among people of all ages. Many individuals are increasingly inclined to establish and maintain social (including romantic) relationships online rather than transitioning them into the offline world.

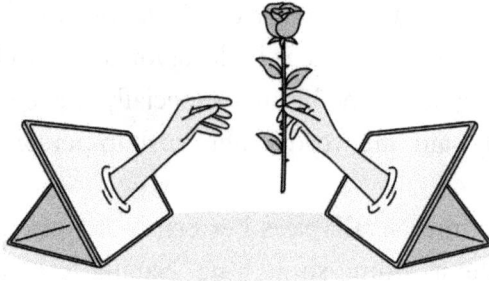

Transition Relationships Offline

Steps:

1. **Practice vulnerability:** Practice being vulnerable with people you know and trust. Being vulnerable can create a safe space where you feel you can express your emotions and thoughts without fear of judgment. This connection is fostered in meaningful connections, and will help you step away from just creating superficial ones. Ponder on what kind of relationship you really want and need. Are you looking for superficial or authentic and real? Practicing vulnerability to foster meaningful connections extends to online connections

too, in the digital world, where vulnerability can be used to work for you, not against you.

2. **Reduce self-judgment and fear:** The online world has given us exposure to so many illusions, including the illusion that people online we see are actually perfect. This illusion is very impactful, however, especially in hurting our self-esteem and confidence. What are the parts that you don't like about yourself and looking down on instead of loving the parts that are so unique about you? No one is perfect, although online shows the perfect side of a person. Who are you comparing yourself to? Is this person real, or are you just getting a single glance into their glamorized and illusionary life?

3. **Don't take it personally:** Sometimes when we are hoping for a meaningful connection with someone, it doesn't always work out. When this happens, it's important not to take it personally and let it negatively affect your ability to be vulnerable and respond to future connections. In the online realm, individuals often don't pause to carefully consider their comments and reactions. You lack insight into their emotional state or intentions, making it unwise to interpret their responses as a personal affront. Whether it's casual remarks or instances of rejection, it's crucial not to internalize these interactions, particularly when you have no prior connection with the individuals involved.

People get rejected and ghosted online more often than in real life. Rejection can serve as a valuable indicator of what lies ahead. Instead of viewing it as a reflection of your self-worth with the belief, "I am not worthy," you can reframe it as a sign that something even more promising awaits you.

If we focused on these three ways to build meaningful relationships online and offline, it would create higher self-confidence and higher self-esteem. *More authentic relationships from our inner self would replace our superficial tendency from the outside that makes us want to be someone else.* Relationships that exist now can come from a real vulnerable you with the use of these three skills now, it's not just for new relationships we create with others.

In the end, the process of building relationships can be intimidating and even daunting, leaving us feeling exposed and vulnerable. This often pushes us towards resorting to online methods such as social media accounts, creating fake profiles, relying on automated AI chats for conversation prompts, and other inauthentic approaches. While these tactics may provide a temporary sense of security, they come at the expense of the lasting sense of safety and fulfillment derived from genuine, meaningful connections with others.

8. Balanced Lifestyle

Kai is always up-to-date with the current social media trends that he sees. He familiarizes himself with current dances, funny videos, and even popular photo aesthetics that are all trending across different platforms. He finds himself investing so much more time in his social media, spends hours posting photos of himself, videoing every minute of his day, keeping his followers updated with every meal he eats, workout routines and latest shoes he purchased. He is obsessed with checking and updating his feed, until his brain is overloaded.

In Kai's attempt to stay popular on people's screens, his entire life is accessible online. His accounts are public, he replies to every comment and message he receives instantly, and posts just about any picture or update he can just to get likes. It makes him feel important. Kai's whole life begins to be online, every detail uploaded on anyone's screen. The pressure of feeling obligated to post his entire life and interact with others online starts to take a toll on Kai's well-being. He feels anxious when he cannot decide on what picture from the 100 pictures he just took to upload or what caption to write, and he wants to silence all his notifications to close off the world from his screen, but feels trapped.

Instead of creating a balance between his life online and his life off the screen, Kai has the illusion that it is the same, that his real life cannot exist without online and vice versa. He is pushed back and forth between two extremes: capturing his entire life online or shutting off the screen for good. These two extremes are in need of balance to create a healthy relationship between Kai and the digital world.

To guide us in creating balance, the following questions to consider will help you think about your identity and life offline, and how you want your identity and life to be portrayed online.

Creating Balance Between Worlds

1. **Who are you?** Have a clarity of who you are before you go online. What are your interests and values? How would you describe yourself to others in person? What qualities do you like most about yourself? Create a clear idea of

how you want to present yourself so you aren't molded by social media and become someone you are not.

2. **Who do you want to be online?** After thinking about who you are offline, think about how much of this you want to convey and expose to the rest of the world. How private do you want to keep your personal life from your publicized life? How much are you willing to let your followers know about you? Do you want online people to know you just as well as the real people in your life?

3. **What is your goal?** When you post your life online, what is the reason that motivates you to do it? Why do you post your life online for others to see? Identifying your goals can act as a filter to help you decide if posting fits the end result you are looking for. Does gaining more followers from posting make you feel powerful? Is your goal to help others by spreading awareness through posting? Are you looking to promote what is important to you?

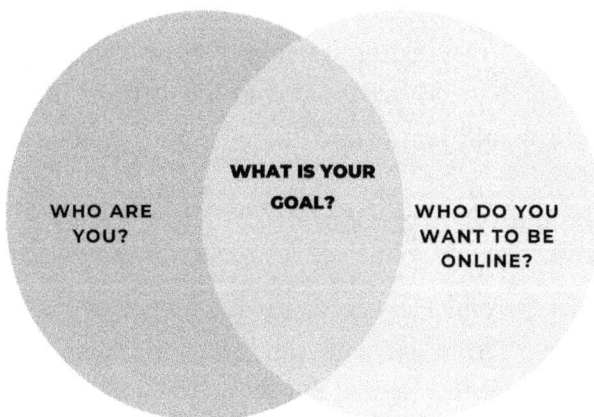

WHO ARE YOU?

WHAT IS YOUR GOAL?

WHO DO YOU WANT TO BE ONLINE?

A balanced lifestyle between our real life and who we are online is increasingly important as we are exposed to new digital creations that can further consume our minds and let us forget about the importance of being offline too. Whether we get stuck picking a filter for photos, using AI photoshop to make us look different, allowing others to view our location, immersing ourselves in AI-driven AR and VR experiences, fostering balance in our lives offline will prevent us from going back and forth between two extremes seen with Kai. Balance guides technology to being a tool that is useful to us, instead of it pushing us into a chaotic state of well-being.

Chapter 10:

A Balanced Tech-Life

Practicing Emotional-Digital Literacy

n the evolution of our digital age, navigating relationships, love, careers, and education requires a skill set that goes far beyond being able to access technology and use it for our benefit. Emotional-digital literacy, including self-awareness, emotion regulation, critical thinking, digital boundaries, digital citizenship, staying present, relationship building, and maintaining a balanced lifestyle, acts as a guide that helps us through the complexities of our tech-driven lives.

Think about the profound impact of emotional-digital literacy on our connections. Making friends and forming romantic relationships online demand a deeper understanding of emotions and mindful use of digital boundaries. These skills become unmatched in value as we build balanced routines for our careers and education that harmonize with the integration of technology into our daily lives. Even in the realm of healthcare, emotional-digital literacy becomes a tool to balance human touch with technological advancements.

During the growth of AI-driven distractions post-pandemic, emotional-digital literacy remains our gateway to the balanced lifestyle we desire. Whether it's algorithms fighting for our attention or virtual voice assistants streamlining tasks, our ability to regulate emotions and set digital boundaries becomes crucial. As we advance as a society, the need to strike a balance between the digital and the real becomes more important than ever.

Practicing emotional-digital literacy is not a straight path journey. Setbacks are inevitable in a world where we constantly encounter technology every minute. Yet, the key to balance lies in using mindfulness to reconnect with our emotional-digital literacy toolbox. It's about finding that balanced lifestyle without completely disconnecting from technology. As we make progress, emotional-digital literacy can be the anchor that keeps us grounded to using our toolbox in the digital era.

In our pursuit of emotional-digital literacy, we don't have to use all the tools we have learned simultaneously. Instead, choose the toolboxes that resonate most with you, ones that light a spark of personal transformation. Much like our lives, acquiring emotional-digital literacy is not a straight pathway, but instead a learning journey that may have some unexpected turns. There is a misconception that emotional-digital literacy comes with age and experience, but this skill set is nurtured through open-mindedness and heightened awareness. Your emotional-digital literacy toolbox thrives on this very awareness, empowering you to navigate the digital world with intention and purpose.

HABIT TRACKER

Practice using emotional digital literacy for 10 days!
Do you notice any difference in your life?

ASSESSING SELF-AWARENESS

REGULATING EMOTIONS

CRITICAL THINKING

DIGITAL BOUNDARIES

DIGITAL CITIZENSHIP

STAY IN THE PRESENT

RELATIONSHIP BUILDING

BALANCED LIFESTYLE

The Emotional Code:
Mastering Communication in the Digital Age of AI

Workbook Companion

N ow that you've completed 'The Emotional Code,' this interactive workbook allows you to reflect and explore the concepts in greater depth. With a series of thought-provoking questions and engaging activities, you'll build upon the knowledge and skills you gained to master communication in the digital age.

Take your time to engage with each one, letting any new insights and emotions that arise fully surface.

The Digital Era: The Role of Technology in Our Lives

Can you recall a personal experience or moment where you felt the direct impact of technology in your daily life, and how did it make you feel?

_____

_____

_____

_____

_____

_____

_____

_____

_____

_____

_____

_____

_____

_____

_____

Chapter 1: Reshaping Realities: Digital Metamorphosis

1. Reflecting on the Digital Transformation

Take a moment to envision a world without the technological advancements we enjoy today. What would you miss the most?

_____

_____

_____

_____

_____

_____

_____

_____

_____

_____

_____

_____

2. The Pandemic's Impact on Tech and Humanity:

When you think about the COVID-19 pandemic and its role in reshaping our reliance on technology, what emotions and realizations come to mind? How did this period affect your digital habits and emotions related to technology?

_____

_____

_____

_____

_____

_____

_____

_____

_____

_____

_____

_____

_____

_____

_____

Chapter 2: Our Life's Source Code: Technology

1. Tech Revolution Reflection:

Think about the various ways technology has transformed different aspects of your life - from love and work to learning and well-being. Can you share a fun or surprising moment when you realized just how deeply technology had integrated into your daily routine? How did this realization make you feel?

_____

_____

_____

_____

_____

_____

_____

_____

_____

_____

_____

_____

2. The Digital Superpower:

Imagine you have the ability to invent a groundbreaking technology that will enhance any aspect of your life. What would you create, and how would it revolutionize your personal journey? How does this futuristic innovation make you excited about the possibilities of technology in your life? The sky is the limit!

_____

_____

_____

_____

_____

_____

_____

_____

_____

_____

_____

_____

_____

Chapter 3: Social Relationships in the Age of Screens

1. The Digital Connection Paradox:

Reflect on your own experiences with online and AI connections, like social media interactions, gaming, etc. Can you recall a moment when you felt deeply connected during a digital interaction, and yet, a sense of emptiness lingered once the screen turned off? What emotions did this paradoxical experience between real and artificial connections in the digital age?

_____

_____

_____

_____

_____

_____

_____

_____

_____

_____

2. Oxytocin vs. Screens:

Imagine a future where screens and digital communication continue to dominate our interactions. How do you envision this affecting our ability to form meaningful in-person connections and experience the warmth of human touch, such as a hug? What emotions arise when considering the potential impact on future generations and their understanding of physical connection and empathy?

_____

_____

_____

_____

_____

_____

_____

_____

_____

_____

_____

_____

_____

Chapter 4: Finding Your Heart Online

1. Swipe Culture Reflection:

Have you ever experienced the "swipe mentality" in your online interactions, either as a quick judge or someone who felt judged? Share a memorable moment or realization related to this culture. How did it impact your perspective on building genuine connections in the digital dating world?

_____

_____

_____

_____

_____

_____

_____

_____

_____

_____

_____

_____

_____

2. Authentic Online Love:

In the world of digital romance, imagine a scenario where technology brings deep, genuine connections rather than superficial judgments. What can we do now to make sure these digital connections bring us happiness and don't make us feel sad or confused? What kind of innovative digital tool or feature would you invent to create this authentic connection?

_____

_____

_____

_____

_____

_____

_____

_____

_____

_____

_____

_____

Chapter 5: The Digital Boost in Our Professions

1. Virtual Work Realities:

Think about your own work experiences. How has technology, especially virtual meetings and remote work, impacted your job and the way you collaborate with colleagues? Has it been more of a blessing or a frustration?

_____

_____

_____

_____

_____

_____

_____

_____

_____

_____

_____

_____

2. The Future of Work:

As technology continues to reshape the professional landscape, what do you see as the biggest challenges and opportunities for your career in the digital age? How do you plan to stand out in a world where AI and global competition are changing the game?

_____

_____

_____

_____

_____

_____

_____

_____

_____

_____

_____

_____

_____

_____

Chapter 6: Education.edu

1. Education's Brave New World:

In a world where education is just a few clicks away, what's the most extraordinary thing you've learned online, and how has it changed your perspective on traditional education? How can we evaluate the trade-offs between experience and convenience in virtual education? Share a story or insight that has left a lasting impact on your educational journey.

_____

_____

_____

_____

_____

_____

_____

_____

_____

_____

_____

_____

2. Balancing AI and Human Teaching:

Can you create a chart highlighting the key qualities you value in human teachers on one side and the advantages of AI and technology in education on the other side?

Qualities in human teachers	Qualities in AI-Driven Teaching
_____	_____
_____	_____
_____	_____
_____	_____
_____	_____

Now, imagine you are an educational innovator – how would you use the insights from this chart to design a groundbreaking learning experience that combines the best of both worlds?

_____

_____

_____

_____

_____

_____

Chapter 7: Wellness, Well–being, and the Web

1. Defining Well-being:

How would you define "well-being," and what aspects of your life do you believe contribute most significantly to your overall well-being?

_____

_____

_____

_____

_____

_____

_____

_____

_____

_____

_____

_____

_____

_____

2. Robo-Care:

How do you personally feel about the idea of replacing traditional, in-person care with 'Robo-Care' for healthcare and mental health support? What potential benefits or drawbacks do you see for yourself in this shift?

_____

_____

_____

_____

_____

_____

_____

_____

_____

_____

_____

_____

_____

Chapter 8: What is Emotional–Digital Literacy?

1. Unplugging from Digital Emotions:

If you had to spend an entire day without any digital devices or technology, how do you think it would impact your emotions and daily routines? What activities or habits would you miss the most, and why?

_____

_____

_____

_____

_____

_____

_____

_____

_____

_____

_____

_____

2. The Digital Pulse of Emotions:

Reflect on a recent experience where technology, such as social media or messaging apps, influenced your emotions or interpersonal relationships. How did you navigate this digital-emotional interaction, and what insights did you gain from it?

_____

_____

_____

_____

_____

_____

_____

_____

_____

_____

_____

_____

Chapter 9: Tool Box: Practicing Our New Strengths Everyday

1. Assessing Self-Awareness:

After a long day, you find yourself engaging in a heated online argument. What emotions are triggered by this online interaction, and how do they affect your well-being?

_____

_____

_____

_____

Reflecting on your digital consumption, what content tends to trigger strong emotional responses, and how can you manage these triggers more effectively?

_____

_____

_____

_____

_____

2.Emotional Regulation:

Think about a recent situation where technology or social media triggered intense emotions. How did you handle these emotions, and what strategies did you use to calm yourself down?

_____

_____

_____

_____

_____

Can you share an experience where you paused before sending a heated online response? How did this pause help you manage your emotions and communication better?

_____

_____

_____

_____

_____

_____

_____

3. Critical Thinking:

In today's digital age, misinformation and fake news are prevalent on social media platforms. Share an experience where you came across information online that seemed questionable or misleading. How did you apply critical thinking to assess its accuracy, and what steps did you take to verify the information before accepting it as true?

_____

_____

_____

_____

Have you ever made impulsive decisions online, such as purchasing or believing information without questioning it? How could critical thinking have guided you differently in those situations?

_____

_____

_____

_____

_____

_____

4. Digital Boundaries:

For some, the thought of setting digital boundaries can be intimidating or even anxiety-inducing. What might be some underlying reasons why people might avoid or resist setting boundaries in the digital age?

_____

_____

_____

_____

_____

Take a moment to examine your own patterns of online behavior and engagement. Are there any signs that you could benefit from setting clearer digital boundaries? How might you go about protecting your emotional health and well-being while navigating the digital realm?

_____

_____

_____

_____

_____

5. Digital Citizenship:

Have you ever encountered or witnessed behavior online that lacked digital citizenship? How did it affect the online community or relationships involved?

_____

_____

_____

_____

_____

_____

_____

_____

_____

_____

_____

_____

_____

_____

6. Staying Present:

Reuben's struggle with staying present during quality time with his girlfriend is a common issue in today's digital age. How can you cultivate mindful engagement with technology to prioritize real-life moments?

_____

_____

_____

_____

_____

_____

Share an experience when you or someone you know found it challenging to stay present due to constant digital distractions. What steps can be taken to overcome this challenge and be more mindful?

_____

_____

_____

_____

_____

_____

7. Relationship Building

Many rely heavily on digital connections to get to know their crush. What are the pros and cons of using social media as a tool for building relationships? Where you hesitated to approach someone you were interested in? How did you handle it?

_____

_____

_____

_____

_____

_____

The chapter discusses the importance of transitioning online relationships to the offline world. Can you share an experience where you successfully made this transition? What challenges did you face, and how did it impact the relationship?

_____

_____

_____

_____

_____

_____

8. Balanced Lifestyle

Reflect on your own online presence and habits. Do you find yourself spending excessive time on social media or other digital platforms? How has it affected your well-being?

Kai becomes consumed by his online life, feeling pressured to post every aspect of his day. Have you ever felt overwhelmed by the need to update your online presence constantly? Or check other friends' or influencers' updates. How did it affect your offline life?

Chapter 10: A Balanced Tech–Life

Examine each one of the aspects connected to AI and the digital world.

How much does AI digital technology empower and improve the following aspects of your well-being in your life?

Rate on a scale of 1 to 5, with 1 indicating no contribution and 5 indicating a very significant contribution:

	1 NONE	2 LITTLE	3 SOME	4 MUCH	5 MOST
Physical Health Diet, exercise, sleep quality, and overall physical fitness.	1	2	3	4	5
Mental Health Emotional resilience, stress management, and psychological well-being.	1	2	3	4	5
Work-Life Balance How your career, job satisfaction, and work-related stress contribute to your well-being.	1	2	3	4	5
Environmental Factors Consideration of your surroundings, access to nature, and how they affect your overall health.	1	2	3	4	5
Spirituality Personal beliefs, values, and practices that enhance your sense of purpose and fulfillment.	1	2	3	4	5
Hobbies and Interests Pursuits, hobbies, or passions that bring joy and satisfaction to your life.	1	2	3	4	5
Social Connections Relationships with family, friends, and community- how they impact your happiness and sense of belonging..	1	2	3	4	5

Appendix

- **Asses: Self-Awareness:** Understanding and recognizing your emotional responses to digital content and interactions.

- **Emotional Regulation:** The ability to manage and control your emotions when engaging with technology, preventing impulsive reactions.

- **Critical Thinking:** Evaluating digital content, information, and interactions with a discerning and thoughtful mindset.

- **Digital Boundaries:** Establishing and maintaining healthy limits on your technology usage to protect your emotional well-being. What do I keep private or what not? Do I answer each message? Do I copy from chatGPT or not? What pictures do I put on dating websites?

- **Digital Citizenship:** Practicing responsible and ethical behavior online, considering the emotional impact on others.Chasing bf/gf/ex/anyone spying on them.

- **Mindful Engagement:** Engaging with technology intentionally and with awareness, rather than mindlessly or compulsively. Resilience: Building the ability to bounce back from negative online experiences or digital setbacks. Do I do it for attention?

- **Relationship Building:** Fostering meaningful connections and relationships in both digital and real-world contexts. Use it to work for you, not against you. (spying after people) vs making connections.

- **Balanced Lifestyle:** Striving for a harmonious integration of technology into your life, ensuring it enhances rather than detracts from your overall well-being.

    - **Balanced Duality:** creating harmony between technology and your life to ensure technology is an enhancement, not an impairing glitch.

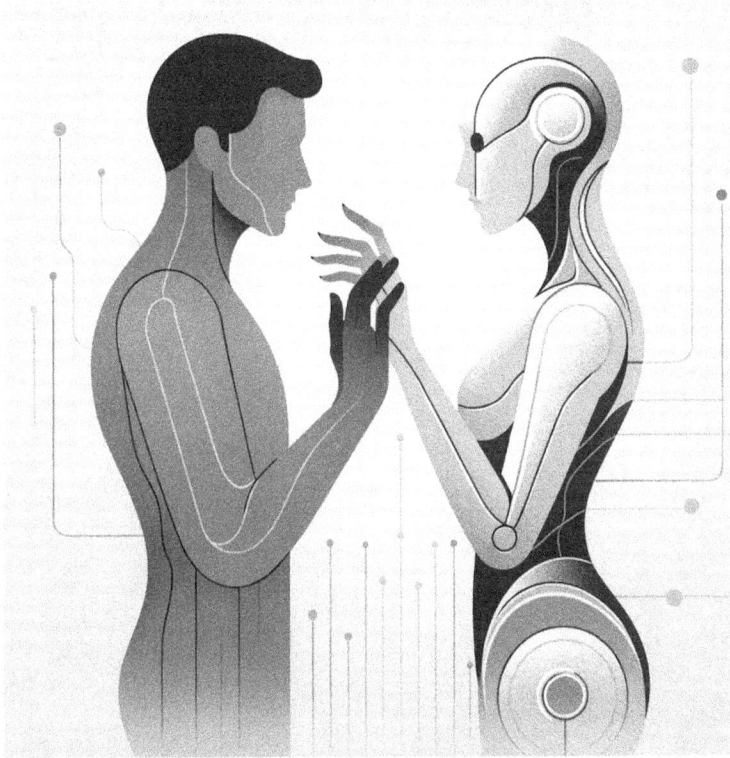

"People will forget what you said,
people will forget what you did,
but people will never forget
how you made them feel."

MAYA ANGELOU